BALCONIES OF TIME

BALCONIES OF TIME

Amit Shankar Saha

Hawakal Publishers

Balconies of Time
Published by Subhra Chakraborty
on behalf of Hawakal Publishers

185, Kali Temple Road, Nimta, Calcutta
700049, India.

Website: www.hawakal.com
Contact: info@hawakal.com

Copyright: Amit Shankar Saha
First edition (Paperback): November, 2017
Printed and bound at S. P. Communications, Calcutta.

All rights reserved. No part of this publication may be reproduced or transmitted (other than for purposes of review/critique) in any form or by any means, electronic or mechanical, including photocopy, recording, or any information storage and retrieval system without prior permission in writing from the publisher or the author, as applicable.

Cover concept & design: Akash Sen

ISBN-13: 978-81-935325-3-9

Price: INR 200/- / US Dollar 9

TIMELESS AESTHETIC EXPRESSIONS

It is common knowledge that the advent and slow evolution of Indian English Poetry can be traced back to the Company poets of the late eighteenth century, thereafter to Henry Louis Derozio, Toru Dutt, Sarojini Naidu and others, all of whom wrote poetry in English, during the days of the British Raj in India.

After India's independence, during the post-colonial period, Indian English poetry evolved from replication and self-fashioning, appropriation and abrogation, characteristics of the colonial period to significantly map a liberated poetic journey that prioritized Indian culture, ethnicity, regional culture, ethnic linguistic patterns, metaphors and images. Nevertheless, the difference between regional language poetry and Indian English poetry, during the post-independence period, was primarily the latter's representation of the culture of the metros, the culture of the cities and suburbs. Indian English poetry therefore exuded a pan-Indian flavour which attracted a pan-Indian readership. Soon after however, Indian English poetry did not remain confined within the geographical contours of contemporary India. Diasporic Indian poets began writing about their homeland through the emotive creation of a series of indelible memories of trauma, loss and longing. So in the twenty-first century and in the era of globalization a paradigmatic shift can be evinced in the writing of Indian English poetry, which is neither just local nor only pan-Indian, for Indian English poetry has now engineered a cultural bridge between the home and the world.

In the ever expanding ripples of Indian English poetry which internalizes the local, national and global intimations of culture, we can often find evidences of the transformations in the urban, suburban and rural culture of India, as we familiarize ourselves with the refreshing new poems that are being written and published in recent times. Interestingly, through the past two or three centuries if not more, the multilingual, multicultural, multi-religious culture of India has consequently ushered in perceptible polyglot skills, cultural pluralism and linguistic diversity. Among educated and privileged classes the use of three languages both for reading and writing is not considered unusual. Also, quite remarkably, the use of an Indian regional language meshed inextricably with the English language for reading, writing and speaking and often the use of English as the language of creative expression and not just communication, is not considered uncommon.

The Indian English poets who began writing around the nineteen fifties onwards, such as P.Lal, Parthasarathy, Arun Kolkatkar, Kamala Das, Nissim

Ezekiel and Eunice Dsouza among many others, demonstrated that the English language for writing poetry was not a constraint but liberated the Indian English poets from binding themselves within the region-specific and culture-specific ambit.

In the last three decades, that is, from the nineties of the twentieth century to the twenty-first century, Indian English poetry has shown significant promise, gusto and power and this has happened primarily because young adults, high school students, college and university students, researchers, young professionals from diverse sectors, have begun to publish their poetry with confidence. The cyber networks and social media have instilled confidence in young poets, who may be teachers, doctors, engineers and journalists, to share their work with the world.

Amit Shankar Saha's debut collection of poems, *Balconies of Time*, emphasizes a poetic spirit that can engage words and rhythm in a felicitous fusion. So the poet's sensitivity and skill in the use of words to create emotive images exhibit a refreshing brilliance of concision and cadence as he writes, "*Some winters are so cold you need to hug a hope for warmth.*" A student, teacher and researcher of Western literature and Indian English Literature, Saha has admirably used the English language with felicity, demonstrating the malleability of the English language, one of its outstanding merits.

The forty-eight poems in Amit Shankar Saha's collection *Balconies of Time,* traverse a wide trajectory, from Awadh to Park Street and Southern Avenue, from Uxbridge to California. The poems also bear the unmistakable stamp of a diligent student of western literature, as some of the poems are titled, "Gyre," "Double Helix," "Cryptology," and "Delilah." "Delilah" ends with the telling line, "*gaze eyeless at Gaza.*" Apart from the rich diversity of content one noticeable feature of Saha's chiselled poems are their brevity, concision and the internal rhythmic nuances that enfold each new thought, each imagined image, each emotive expression that blends sense and sensibility seamlessly. Amit Shankar Saha's debut volume of poems, *Balconies of Time,* will surely inspire newer generations of poets to play with words meaningfully, in order to create timeless aesthetic expressions.

Sanjukta Dasgupta
Calcutta
October 31, 2017

ACKNOWLEDGEMENTS

Some of these poems have been published in *Ann Arbour Review*, *Tuck Magazine*, *Oddball Magazine*, *Harbinger Asylum*, *Duane's PoeTree*, *I am Not a Silent Poet*, *Dissident Voice*, *The Cauldron*, *Hakara*, *Wordweavers*, *Learning and Creativity*, and *Solitary Window*. I'm thankful to the editors of those journals and magazines. The poem "Damning the Sky" was inspired by a quote of Agha Shahid Ali mentioned in the poem and Bob Dylan's "The Answer is Blowing in the Wind." The poem "Dances in Vacuum" was inspired by songs like Frank Sinatra's "Strangers in the Night," John Denver's "Annie's Song," and Maurice Jarre's Lara's Theme from the movie, *Doctor Zhivago*. Some of these poems were written in response to prompts provided on Facebook groups "The Significant League" and "The Missing Slate" during National Poetry Writing Month and Global Poetry Writing Month. The poem "How to Kill a Tree" was written on a prompt given by Kaafiya Milaao which was the first line of a Gieve Patel poem.

I owe my thanks for the title of the book and inspiration for the poems to fellow poet, Ananya Chatterjee. I am also grateful to another fellow poet, Kushal Poddar, for all his guidance. Thanks also go to Anindita Bose and Sufia Khatoon, my fellow co-founders of Rhythm Divine

Poets group, youngsters like Sana Mohammed and Swasti Jaiswal and seniors like Sharmila Ray, Sanjukta Dasgupta, Nabina Das and Somali Panda for their support. I also thank Barnali Saha and Sharanya Bhattacharya, who encouraged me during crucial parts of my poetic career. I also owe my thanks to Andrew Bellon (I'm sad, he is no more) and Barbara Maat, who edited some of the poems. I acknowledge the contributions of the various poetry groups, both in the virtual and the real worlds, which helped to hone my poetic talent. And last but not the least, special thanks go to my teacher, Steve Menezes, my brother, Jyoti, and his wife, Indu, and my family and close friends for their constant support and belief in me.

I thank the entire team of Hawakal Publishers for bringing my dream into a reality by publishing my maiden collection of poems.

CONTENTS

Awadh	13
The River and I	14
Unseason	15
Silhouettes	16
A Girl Writes About Breaking Sleep	17
The Last Tea	18
Impressions from a Train	19
Gyre	21
Aleppo	22
Delilah	24
Fist of Imagination	25
Double Helix	26
Phobias	27
Gravid	28
Damning the Sky	29
Imagined Dream	30
Silverfish	31
Silent Night	32
Re-Collection	33
Rippleless	34
Cryptology	35
Fog	36
Unforgetfulness	37
Unwakefulness	38

Balconies of Time	39
After Ecstasy	40
Dances in Vacuum	41
The Last Riverine Civilization	42
The One I Should Not Name	43
Discovering Guilt	44
Dispersal	45
Body	46
Sometimes in California	47
Uxbridge	48
Ruislip	49
Little Hands	50
Rara Avis	51
Some Place Else	52
Park Street	53
Gariahat	54
Southern Avenue	55
Under the Quilt	56
Birch	57
Lost Verdancy	58
A Secret of Forests	59
Heartbreak of the Lost Earth	60
Coral	61
How to Kill a Tree	62

Awadh

The nights of Awadh are famous for poetry.
Sometimes the night waits at a door to say a few
Words of Ghalib or Rumi in a soft whisper.
Sometimes the boisterous laughter of the night
Can be heard across the windows lit with oil lamps,
Whose fragrance permeates the walls under the moon,
Who keeps vigil as a companion will do.
Sometimes the night gets intoxicated and walks
The lanes in faintly heard music of *gazal*s
And slowly fades in drowsiness into the dawn.
The days of Awadh are filled with the languor of
The chess players contemplating the movements of
Armies on the chequered board as the smell from
The kitchen stoves fill the air with thoughts of a feast.
Then the day gets tired climbing and comes down
Like a drop of tear descending from your eye,
And again the night stumbles in unsteadily,
Like a poem disinterred from one's memory.

The River and I

The rivered rocks talk to me
about a silted sleep
where a Radha-coloured flood
submerged a lichen dream.
The sadness of river banks
stems from unfooted steps
where a Shyam-coloured drought
left the river bereft.
What if *Shravan* revisits
and again makes us wet
and fleeting memories hug
our bodies like drenched clothes?
What if we meet and pretend
that we had never met?

Unseason

In this unseason season
it is inauspicious
to start anything new.
A bunch of *Nilkanth*
colours with blasphemy
all my closet transgressions.
I, a flower-picking girl,
hide behind my stealing eyes
a month of stolens leaves.
My worship of the buds
is a secret which bursts
a blush of ripe sacrilege.
O *Bhadra*!
Be gentle on me.

Silhouettes

I imagine the life of that girl
in a short-sleeve three-quarter dress,
who watches countless trains pass by
while being stranded on her balcony.
I name her Nayantara and
imagine that she never saw
all those trains carrying dead bodies
of all those partition refugees.
History has been so kind to her.
So, while rushing back on train when I see
in the fields silhouettes of crucified trees,
I let her be, I let her be.

A Girl Writes about Breaking Sleep

a girl writes about breaking sleep
these arthritic trees
rheumatoid moments
plantain parades
wanton journeys
passing platforms
doppler passengers
a grid that holds electric wires
a wet night dress hung out to dry
an old man's struggle with lock and key
the white of *kaash phool* in the grey of dusk fields
dim light burns dim day's end
shadow of a train on houses by the tracks
a girl sitting on a window sill
with her back to the world
what will happen
will depend on
what will happen

The Last Tea

After the funeral of the leaves
I see a bird on the rock,
a butterfly, a river,
sound of gurgling water
fading as I leave.
Thoughts become dragonflies,
fly over trees.
Who shall come back to them,
like a squirrel amongst the greens,
if not me?
Too much is left behind
and the smell of what never has been.
The lost smoke from the oven
and the last tea.

Impressions from a Train

As I travel by train
I see through the window
flickering lives of others.

Countless coaches pass by,
shimmering past their eyes.
Bent over for ages sow seeds.

Racks of crops line the tracks.
Palms. Fronds. Plantains.
All for a while.

Those men who work on rails,
fixing lines with iron girders.
Those cranes in the fields.

Audacity of a bird
sitting on a fishplate.
Chimney of a brick kiln.

Crossing engines.
Vending lives of others.
Planks of concrete consciousness.

Chips of abandoned sleep.
Cows in pale yellow water.
Red earth. Merging tracks.

A woman searching for thoughts.
An unscheduled stop.
All getting lost.

Gyre

Today I sit to write
the last poem of the year.
Words queue to climb
the anthill of poetry.
They mate with each other
to give birth to meaning.
Some words remain
isolated,
alone in a line,
trying to match the meter
or cover the syllables
or demanding a deep breath
and a slow aspiration.
Such a word becomes the pivot
on which spins the poem
in a gyre.

Aleppo

I do not love you birch
and I have learnt to lie.
Your yellowed leaves I keep
in pages of poetry.
Between my pretensions
I ecocriticize.

And if I cry I say
I cry for Syria.
Aleppo's children are
all dearer to me.
Their blasted past mirrors
denial of history.

On the blackboard of life
so much chalk dust we wipe.
But in the palimpsest
everything is inside.
(Hidden) In the layers
live all those who have died.

So, the fall in autumn
and the death in December,
all, all I will deny.
I will seal the ceilings,
the floorboards too and hope
there remains a crack or two.

Remember Bamian,
we were the Buddhas there,
now there the desert dwells.
Look birch, how the dust flies
in Aleppo and dies
all intertextual.

Delilah

Delilah,
why don't you now
cut my locks of memories too?
In the dark they all come back,
every bit...
dense as the night.
When all the lights go to sleep
we grow our cropped hair
once again long.
The dust of your days
settles on my eyes
layers on layers.
But in your starved mind
philistine thoughts betray
all thoughts of us.
Good that my eyes are gouged out
for don't we all today
gaze eyeless at Gaza?

Fist of Imagination

Last month
everything came with the floods.
This month
my feet get filled with silt.
It rises with sap
up my veins
and bursts into clouds
in my brain.

"Every spring every wound
becomes a mother."
Who said that?
Every spring every moon
becomes a lover,
every star, the other.
Brother, will you
lower the sky a bit?

I once imagined
travelling to the northeast.
It took so much of imagination.
Bullets are swift,
you can't see them.
Between silted feet
and lowered sky, there is
a fist of imagination.

Double Helix

Read your mother's poem,
You have her genes.
My mother does not write.
On world poetry day
She cooked, watched TV
And that was it.
I never asked her
Whether she likes doing
What she does.
She has grown in her duties
And made them her home.
She never had words
As comfort zone.
I have my mother's genes,
I am not a poet
And this is not a poem.
At the crossroad
This will not pay for my coffee.
It is still the seventies
And we are still unborn.
In our double helixes
Genes turn left and right.
Which of our mothers will
Now become a Naxalite?

Phobias

The Suicide Bomber in My Head
Three old drinks clink at a pub.
Hands search for an absent vintage.
In the cellar of phobias
Lie bottled my death, your death.

Twin Towers
Tonight I could not sleep
in the noise of your dream
flying into my head.
See how it replaces
all the phobias of life
with the philia of death.

Your Xenophobia
In which direction the birds fly?
What if I love you in that direction?
While you gather phobias from the clouds,
I shall keep unfolding the sky.

Gravid

Head down I crouch in a fluid-filled sac.
All my movements are constrained within a
translucent membrane. It is dark inside
this strong protective purse. Until my hands
render a schism and rip the surface
asunder. The water breaks into a
rupture and I pass through a caved canal.
The cave contracts, my head palpates, while I
at the cervix emerge to birth and breathe.
And while my amniotic fluid dries,
my umbilical cord collapses, I
start to forget my state of dependence.
I am no longer my placental self.
Terrified of my own freedom I cry
and at every breath my innocence dies.
Everything begins when everything ends.

Damning the Sky

There's no answer blowing in the wind,
Summer's not the summer that has been,
It doesn't even rain inside.
Inside the night a mid-day sun,
Inside the day a darkened night,
Birds hide at dawn,
Chirps muffled in humidity,
On sweaty skin air sticks like memory.
Shahid says, "It rains as I write this,
Mad heart, be brave."
I look around the parched land,
It is like nostalgia,
Nothing alive will sprout out,
In the desert of dead deeds
I can plough a furrow,
Plant seeds of tomorrow,
And wait for the missing rains.
Shahid, it doesn't rain any more,
Mad heart, how brave can you still be?
Someone must have dammed the sky.

Imagined Dream

Saw a picture of yours,
It was January,
You looked so beautiful.

In the dark room of my dreams
I develop an alternate reality,
Where it is still January
And I am in the picture.

And there is no picture,
For the moment did not pass,
And the months did not progress.

A world recreated in the reverse,
Where we became playmates
And the bard did not sing
That our playtime was over.

In that imagined world,
In that imagined time,
Suppose we fell asleep.

What dreams we would have dreamt?
Suppose that dreamt future is now
And I am really in the picture –
How do I awake from an imagined dream?

Silverfish

As I lie on my bed
And the night eats me up
A silverfish comes to my rescue.

A long lost thought that lies
Folded in the cupboard
Seeks a sudden breath of fresh air.

A book of memories
Kept undusted for years
Seeks an unseasonal dusting.

The room becomes yellow
And I know it's been long
Really long ago...

Silverfish come along
And make me love the night
While the stars fade out at twilight.

Silverfish! Silverfish!
Do not scurry and hide
Listen to what fairies confide.

Shh... Listen...
"If his fate is to get burnt
In trying to catch the stars,
Then so be it, so be it."

Silent Night

The night, a hymn of silence,
keeps me awake
with its metronome.

Far away protests rise
like Remedios, the beauty,
into the 4 p.m. sky.

We did not go to that restaurant
where silverfishes swim
and no one remembers.

Tonight I take out from the cupboard
my boxes of false nostalgias
and smell their moth-eaten velvet covers.

People still protest
against atrocities committed...
They have nothing to do.

If you are living in this poem
you will come to the eighteenth line
to discover solitude.

Re-Collection

Your eyes become fish
and my hands become depth,
I dip in to fetch
the sky caught in the net,

the moon becomes a lie
and stars mirages,
my hands cuddle the bones
of silverfishes' breath,

sand and shells all sleep
when night wakes me up,
a fisherman resurrects
to hook the flooding death.

Rippleless

Rains sweep in a memory
on my corrugated sleeplessness.
A noise crawls
in the forest of the night.
Stray dogs bark
at my room of wakefulness.
Tonight you become thin
like dementia.
I send a sound to the mountain,
nothing echoes back.
How difficult it is to breathe
frozen blocks of air?
In the sea of desire
your thoughts skim
like figures of speech.
On the plateau of friendship
I drop a pebble
and wait for no ripple.

Cryptology

Two black boats float
under your irises,
like hieroglyphics,

in the sea of your face,
write a crow's feet script
with the creeks of your eyes.

Perhaps everything stands
still in a doldrum
of your low pressure

or the storms of the past
churn a cryptogram
of pain in your chest.

The green of your night
does not die or fade,
sleeplessness sails

with ballast of bags
filled with work and vigil
and no dreams are made.

Fog

We walk into fog
and vanish with rain.
Clouds become waves
on the coast of night.
The sun with patient breath
waits to exhale the day.
On the shore of our pain
a dream builds a castle,
where each hour at the door
like the tide trespasses.
Lives ebb and flow in words,
silence screams in shadows.
On tops of hills
the eyes become the sage.

Unforgetfulness

Remember that day
You had a pimple under your nose,
Today I have it on my face.
Your mark has now faded,
Mine too will soon fade
And nothing will stay.
Nothing ever stays, nothing.

Remember that day
And all the other days.

The fish ate my ring
So I try to catch
The fish of your eyes
Fretting on your face,
Swimming at a depth,
Rising to surface
And nothing ever fades…nothing.

Unwakefulness

My body a boat
Filled with holes of tiredness
Sinks deep into sleep

Your memory a cargo
Lies on the sea bed -
A sunken treasure it seems

The unbecoming
Of ever falling asleep -
The brine of the sea

All the mermaids gather there
To mourn and to weep
For what I lost in my dreams

Balconies of Time

on one balcony of time
I once lingered,
a slow afternoon

>topples gently
>into an evening,
>mild wetness of the rays

dries into darkness,
soon I slip into
another lazy balcony,

>a lump of waiting
>grips my breath,
>where did I leave you,

on which balcony of time,
there's laughter in the grills,
grins in the blinds,

>moon tans lie sprawled
>where I had left you
>on one balcony of time

After Ecstasy

When I shiver in fear
a blanket of indifference
comes to my warm rescue,
reminding me of summer
when I was bold, you were bold
and there was no trembling,
when we cupped in our palms
so much light that the rays
thought they belonged there
and all darkness was sent
to the basement of indifference
where there is always winter.
Today my hands hold darkness,
I am getting used to the cold.

Dances in Vacuum

There's something in the night
And I'm the pumpkin in the patch
Whose slice you have eaten
And exposed the hollow inside.
There's a hollow in the spoon,
Which can feed the whole earth,
Yet our dream children die young
All hungry at birth.
There's a hollow in the forest
Which the night cannot fill
And the sleepy blue ocean
Walks sleepy blue still.
There a hollow in the strangers,
Hollow in their glances
Lurking in the faded corners
With folded hemline of chances.
There's a hollow in the sun,
A hollow in the sun,
There's the burning inside
And no healing in helium.
There's something in the night
And I'm the pumpkin in the patch
And there's a hollow in the moon,
Where we bury our love,
Where I play Lara's theme
And my hollow dances in vacuum.

The Last Riverine Civilization

A bit of the end escapes
And masquerades as me

Nothing lasts except
What exists within

Swallows of the lost
Riverine civilization

Fly from the gut to the heart
Along the river of feelings

Traverse the body of air
Where you are still breathing

The One I Should Not Name

Remembering your collar bone:
Just below your canopy chin
hides your collar bone;
two protrusions under the skin
like two hot eruptions
under a cold ocean.

Remembering your handbag:
You put everything in there;
in the yellow chambers
your hands search for coins,
pen, pad, perhaps lipstick too
and a bit of emotion.

Discovering Guilt

Imagine me making love to you
And you whimpering in ecstasy,
Your body I peel like an orange
And your eyes an inflorescence split in two,
Your breasts I suckle like a hot day
And your breath I take in kisses askew,
Your legs careen on me like cantilevers
And I remain suspended like particulate matter,
Your navel quivers like a seismic center
And fills with quakes the sinning quilt,
Imagine, imagine also all the guilt.

Dispersal

When the moon
makes love
to the earth,
kissing her
all over
with her light,
pulling her
to her side,
until the
night fades
into a
dispersing dawn,
we wake up
in cities of
distances,
filled with
atoms of
orgasms,
all differences,
indifferences
dissolve,
for atoms
make up
everything.

Body

My body, a being alien,
transpires from an aperture.
On the dust-laden leaf of life
a stomata palpitates.
Your body, antipodal,
cannot be seen through the earth.
Crust, mantle, core quake
incessant.
Bodies of clouds cause no rain.
Words in my pen
become bodies in shrouds.
My body has a mind.
My body can think.
My body has cells.
Each cell imprisons me.
Each cell dies.
Within, I expire.
Become a memory of myself.
A body in the mind.
Your mind opens,
lets in a body of nostalgia.
Organs unite,
a frozen metaphor in time.
Our bodies become forgotten rain,
pours like amnesia.

Sometimes in California

It's cold, very cold
    at an altitude.
Sometimes I cannot see
    the whiteness of the snow.
Your black gloves burrow
    in your dark tresses.
Your black sunlit eyes
    hide behind a wink.

Your bohemian boots travel
Alone in a dream territory.

Sometimes it's the hair,
    dark and disheveled.
And the dark eyes
    unexplored, uncharted,
A depth within you.

Sometimes I cannot see
    the river Carmel
when you are in the foreground,
    so beautiful.

Sometimes it's too often,
Sometimes sometimes.

Uxbridge or This Frozen English Summer

See how the children run!
Memory freezes a summer
and a day. The moment
doesn't get tired out
into futility. Nothing
should thaw this summer day
and wash down our children's
growing up years. Nothing.

This refrigerated summer
memory will not grow.
It will not pass out of
school and college. It will
stay uneducated. It will
not learn a lesson or
earn a living. It will
stay a pauper. Always.

This summer day, frozen
in time like a crystal,
will blind our eyes one day.
And the lasers of the future
will break the crystal cataracts
into infinite pieces of
memories dispersing in the
aged air, everywhere.

Ruislip or Dangerous Faith

in Lido
your dangerous faith
a kite, the sky
and the hands
the hands raised
the bay
runs in the garden
sleeps in the air
watches the water
swims in the bed
dangerous faith
in Lido
night becomes
a tired day
everything comes online
time and space
and matter
I touch myself
my hair, my eyes
and feel
your hair, your eyes
in a dangerous faith
everything becomes
matter

Little Hands

When the weight of the sky
bends my shoulders
and the stars and planets
prop on my will,
we don't sit across a table
wiped clean by little hands.

One little hand squirms inside me,
one little hand in you,
so many moons we did not meet
lie lodged on their fingertips,
blackened enamels with mud
of the road we did not walk.

Little hands…
we never procreated,
they squirm in us and none
shall try to fly by the nets,
their paring nails will not free
any crescents in the sky.

Two little hands collect leftovers
and we left them over there.

Rara Avis

It left a hole in the sky
When it disappeared,
Rara avis.

A crowd of silence
Assembled for the sight.
My own body of silence
Too ambled from the bed
Towards the window ledge.
The lights from far and high
Climbed down the flights of air
And gathered on the earth
To mourn the rare bird.

One day I too shall pass
And leave a hole somewhere,
It may be your heart, perhaps,
And may not be the sky.

Some Place Else

Last night you
at Someplace Else,
having a drink
with a friend.
Tonight I
drink a spirit
of unrequitedness,
glass shivers at my sip.
Is this the rim
that touched your lips?
Under the surface
of my spirit
a farmer boy
tries to speak.
His mouth filled
with dead snakes,
his eyes swell
and swim with loss.
Waiter, please,
how much my drink cost?

Park Street

A blue gypsy skirt seeks
hollow beings in Park Street.
Colours of countdown
stop traffic of time.
At the book store
no dumb-waiters wait
for requisitions of memory.
At the eateries
queue chunks of cosmos.
So many nebulas
drown in the Olypubs.
There is no abracadabra
in the black holes I bring
to the galaxy in Park Street.

Gariahat

That day we flew over
the island of Gariahat.
The flyover licked us
and we were lifted up
in incredible lightness
of being in love.

Tonight you fly over my head,
memories levitate quick from the dead.

That day I bought at Gariahat
one day in the life of us.
That day I got with love
the inheritance of loss for free.

Tonight there is festivity,
the island becomes the sea.

Southern Avenue

The streets were flooded
with nostalgia.
We swam past Menoka
to Southern Avenue.
We learnt to sleep
with eyes wide open.
We learnt to breathe
inside déjà vu.
If you slit my throat
you will still find
membranes of remembrance
in the gills of the past
when we were fishes with
lateral lines of love.

Under the Quilt

When I was a child
I used to build my house
Under the quilt.

From under the quilt
I used to hear
The chirpings of
Crows and sparrows
And sounds of utensils.

From under the quilt
I used to hear
My grandmother
Calling Lado Gopal
From the courtyard.

Under the quilt
It was all sound and warm
And never winter.

Birch

Hello birch!
How are you?
I talk to the tree outside.
I was a toddler then
when it was planted.
Today its branches spread
into my soul.
This December nineteen
I wake up from a dream,
rub my floating eyes
sticky with sleep,
find the fog of time
thick with waiting,
search for the birch outside,
grab the girth of missing.
Some winters are so cold
you need to hug a hope
for warmth
or discover the tree
within.

Lost Verdancy

Post autumn the oak sees
the ochre leaf languishing.
The winter wind
will take it where—
the wise oak thinks—
the foolish leaf.
The foolish leaf
dare not think
for its dried up veins
fear climate change
when the world will sink
in the flood of might-have-beens,
when the oak will be ark
and the leaf will be life.

A Secret of Forests

In the autumn of detachment
I cling to flowers, fruits and leaves,
In the forest of your secrets
You leave a secret to a tree.

While loitering in that forest
I stumble on an ashen bough,
I find the birch who you said
Is freer than you and me.

But has she ever hugged you birch?
Wish your autumn arms hug her back?
For every flower, fruit or leaf you shed
Leaves a cicatrix in your heart.

Heartbreak of the Lost Earth

In the wilderness of Binsar
something gets lost in transition.
All the trees leaf through the forest
in vain search for the lost object.
At night there is sound of heartbreak
amidst the beating of silence.
All the grasses stay up sleepless
listening all night to the earth's quake.
In gulps and moans the world laments,
under our feet grows estrangement.

Coral

It looks like a branch
of a tree. This part of a reef,
colony of calicles,
marine, sessile, invertebrate,
polypless calcium carbonate.
It came from Maldives.
Inside its numerous pores
once plant-like cells made
their home. Day and night
salt water made visits.
Now the limestone skeleton
has no zooxanthellae.
Your coral pores are holes,
hollow, no longer home.

How to Kill a Tree

It takes much time to kill a tree.
First you have to stop communicating.
The more you communicate
The more it flowers.
Stop the blush on the petals.
Then block it
So that, come storm or wind,
The leaves do not fly to your door.
Then, for god's sake,
Stop meeting it.
Every time you meet a tree
Its roots grow deeper.
Then spread slander about the tree,
About how its branches grew
Without your permission.
Then wait.
Waiting is essential,
For the tree will uproot itself.
Once it has tasted blood
It will not be satisfied with water.
It will wrench itself from the earth,
Vomit all the sap.
The tree will become a tiger.
Then all you have to do
Is to take out a gun and shoot it.
Or, if you want a real slow death,
Send it to a sanatorium.

Madness is next to lovelessness
And nobody wants an insane tree
In the backyard.

www.ingramcontent.com/pod-product-compliance
Lightning Source LLC
Chambersburg PA
CBHW031502040426
42444CB00007B/1174